CENGAGE Learning

Novels for Students, Volume 20

Project Editors: Ira Mark Milne and Timothy Sisler **Editorial**: Anne Marie Hacht, Maikue Vang

Rights Acquisition and Management: Edna Hedblad, Sheila Spencer, Ann Taylor **Manufacturing**: Rhonda Williams

Imaging: Lezlie Light, Mike Logusz, Kelly A. Quin **Product Design**: Pamela A. E. Galbreath

Product Manager: Meggin Condino

For more information, contact
Thomson Gale
27500 Drake Rd.
Farmington Hills, MI 48331-3535
Or you can visit our Internet site at

corrected in future editions.

ISBN 0-7876-6943-1
ISSN 1094-3552

Printed in the United States of America
10 9 8 7 6 5 4 3 2 1

The Phantom of the Opera

Gaston Leroux 1910

Introduction

Gaston Leroux's novel *The Phantom of the Opera*, first published in 1910, remained a perennial favorite throughout the twentieth century and into the early 2000s. It was adapted to several popular motion pictures and into one of the most successful stage musicals of all time. Its main character, Erik, is a romantic figure whose appeal reaches across different cultures and times. He is a sensitive soul, an accomplished composer and musician whose great unfinished work, *Don Juan Triumphant*, is described as breathtakingly beautiful by the one person he allows to hear it; he is an object of pity, whose face has been disfigured from birth, causing him to hide behind a silk mask; and he is hopelessly in love with a young woman whom he can never seriously hope will love him back. At the same time, he a dangerous, menacing figure, lurking in the hidden catacombs beneath the opera house and blackmailing those who will not bow to his whims. He can hear things said in privacy and can create catastrophes that might or might not be the accidents that they seem to be.

Like other precursors of modern superheroes, such as the Hunchback of Notre Dame and Frankenstein's creature, Erik balances sympathy with horror, admiration with revulsion. Set in one of the most beautiful buildings in Europe, this story of the love triangle between the phantom, the young peasant-born opera singer he loves, and the dashing viscount who she loves, was written as a thriller, and it continued to excite the imaginations of readers into the twenty-first century.

Author Biography

Gaston Leroux was born in Paris on May 6, 1868, a month before his parents, Dominique Alfred Leroux and Marie Bidault, were married. His father was a public works contractor. After Gaston was born, his parents went on to have two more sons and a daughter.

Gaston Leroux went away to school when he was twelve, graduating with honors at age eighteen. He then went to Caen to study law. In the meantime, his mother died, and his father died soon after Leroux turned twenty. As head of the household, he returned to Paris, where he reluctantly finished studying to be a lawyer, passing the tests required for his license. He preferred writing, however, and began covering trials for smaller papers, which led, in 1893, to a full-time position as a reporter for *Le Matin*. Tremendously successful as a newspaper reporter, he stayed at *Le Matin* for nearly thirteen years. It was an exciting life of global travel, for which he became a celebrity. Soon after he married Marie Lafranc, he realized that the marriage was a mistake; they separated, but she refused to grant him a divorce. He fell in love with another woman, Jeanne Cayatte, and they had a son together, although they were not able to marry until Marie Lafranc died in 1917.

His journalistic career ended suddenly, in 1907, when, after his return from covering a volcano eruption, he sought to relax with a few days of vacation time: his editor ordered him to go out on another assignment, and he spontaneously quit. Having already published one minor novel, he turned to writing fiction. From 1907 until his death in 1927, he published thirty-three novels, as well as twelve short stories and six screenplays.

Leroux died suddenly, unexpectedly, of natural causes on April 27, 1927.

Preface

In the Preface to *The Phantom of the Opera*, the book's narrator tells of the methods he used to research the legend of the phantom. Writing roughly thirty years after the events conveyed in the novel, he tells of his research in the library at the Paris Opera house; his interviews with people who were present at the time; his reliance on the memoirs of one of the opera's directors at that time; and his own study of the opera house.

Chapters 1–5

The first three chapters take place on the night that the old opera directors are retiring and turning over the directorship to Armand Moncharmin and Firmin Richard. While the performers are preparing for the night's show, several of the dancers claim to have seen the phantom. In the basement, Joseph Buquet, the chief stagehand, is found hanged.

At the retirement party, all attention is drawn to the mature, nuanced performance of Christine Daaé, previously an obscure understudy. Raoul de Chegny, attending the opera with his older brother, Count Phillippe de Chegny, falls in love with Christine. When she faints, Raoul pushes his way into the crowd in her dressing room and tells her that he is the little boy who chased her scarf into the sea. After the room is cleared, he listens out-side the door and hears a male voice talking with her inside, saying that he has made her a star.

The retiring directors tell the new directors about the phantom and his demands: he is to have Box 5 always left available to him, and he is to have 20,000 francs paid to him each month. Moncharmin and Richard think this is a joke, and they rent Box Five. Soon after they receive a letter from the phantom, expressing his displeasure about his rules being broken.

Chapters 6–10

The novel gives background information. Christine traveled as a child with her father, an accomplished violinist, settling in the French seaside town of Perros-Guirec. It was there that she first met Raoul de Chegny when her scarf blew into the water, and he dived in to retrieve it. They were separated until he saw her on the stage at the opera.

Christine sends a note to Raoul, telling him to meet her in Perros. When he arrives, she is mysterious and aloof. She explains that the voice he heard in her dressing room was the Angel of Music, whom her father said would watch over her. Raoul follows her to the cemetery at midnight, where, at the tomb of her father, he hears violin music. The next day, he is found unconscious at the tomb, having been attacked by a mysterious cloaked figure with a face like a blazing skull.

Messrs. Richard and Moncharmin investigate Box 5 and are convinced that the whole phantom story is a hoax. They receive a note insisting that *Mme.* Giry be rehired; that Christine be given the lead in *Faust*; and that Box 5 be left abandoned: otherwise, the performance will be cursed. Instead, they hire a new box attendant, give the lead role to Carlotta, and sit in Box 5 themselves. During the performance, Carlotta's voice croaks like a frog's, and the house chandelier drops onto the audience, hurting dozens and killing the woman hired to replace *Mme.* Giry.

Christine disappears after that performance. Hearing that she has been seen riding in a carriage at night in the Bois de Boulogne, Raoul goes there and sees her ride past. She sends him a note, telling him to meet her at a masked ball at the opera house, and what costume to wear. He meets her at the ball, but lurking about there is also a mysterious figure wearing a feathered costume and skull mask. Christine tells Raoul that she cannot see him any more, and when he follows her to her dressing room he sees her disappear into her mirror.

Chapters 11–16

The next day, Raoul goes to *Mme.* Valerius, who is Christine's guardian, and Christine is there, acting as if nothing had happened the night before. She says that she loves Raoul but cannot see him any more.

When he tells her that he must leave within a

month, Christine agrees to a secret engagement with Raoul. She explains to him that the phantom, Erik, is in love with her and insanely jealous and that he is dangerous. She leads Raoul to the roof of the opera house, assuming that Erik cannot hear them talk there. She tells him about being fooled by Erik into thinking that he was the Angel of Music her father talked about, about being held in the basement by the phantom, about listening to his beautiful violin playing and then removing his mask and seeing his grotesque, death-like face. She explains that he finally agreed to let her go hoping to win her love freely. While on the roof, they have a feeling that they are being watched. The next day, Raoul talks with his brother, Philippe, and tells him that he is running away with Christine; Philippe does not approve.

Media Adaptations

- The 1925 silent film version of *The*

Phantom of the Opera was one of the first horror films ever made and remains one of the most influential movies in film history. Lon Chaney Sr. played Erik, the phantom, and Mary Philbin played Christine. The film was directed by Rupert Julian. It was re-released in 1929, with edits and a new score. Both versions are available on DVD in a package called *The Phantom of the Opera— The Ultimate Edition*, from Image Entertainment.

- A second movie was made in 1943, with Claude Rains and Nelson Eddy. This one used all of the sets from the original silent film and augmented them with sound and color. It is available on DVD from Universal.

- The version of this story that is perhaps most familiar to late twentieth-century and twenty-first century audiences is the musical version that debuted at Her Majesty's Theater in London on October 9, 1986, and as of 2004 was still running. The music is by Andrew Lloyd Weber, and the lyrics are by Charles Hart and Richard Stilgoe. By the early 2000s it had been in more than fifty major theaters worldwide and had won more than ninety major awards.

- In 1989, a theatrical motion picture version of *The Phantom of the Opera* was released, starring Robert Englund and Jill Scholen. It is available on videocassette and DVD from Columbia Tristar.

- In 1990, Tony Richardson directed a miniseries of the phantom story for USA network, featuring Charles Dance, Burt Lancaster, and Teri Polo. It is available on DVD from Image Entertainment.

- An unabridged audio reading of this book, read by Barrett Whitener, is available for download from Audible.com.

The following night, in the middle of a performance, the lights go out at the opera. When they come on again, Christine is missing from the stage.

Chapters 17–21

The managers have locked themselves in their office, trying to figure out how the phantom could have changed an envelope of money to counterfeit bills. *Mme.* Giry explains that she switched envelopes and put the real bills into M. Richard's coat pocket, so they pin an envelope of cash into his pocket, only to find, soon after hearing of Christine's disappearance, that the envelope is mysteriously empty.

The Persian, a mysterious figure who has been seen around the opera house, stops Raoul from telling the police about Erik. He leads Raoul to Christine's dressing room and shows him the mechanism by which she appeared to disappear into her mirror. Then he leads Raoul into the cellars of the opera house.

Walking through the cellars, they pass the furnaces and the opera's rat catcher leading a small army of rats to their doom, but they do not see the phantom.

Chapters 22–26

These chapters are told as passages from the Persian's written account of that night. He leads Raoul to a secret panel that will drop them into Erik's house from the cellar above it, without having to cross the lake that he rowed Christine across. They land, however, in a room called the torture chamber and are trapped there. Erik, demanding that Christine agree to marry him, hears them in there and turns the chamber on: bright electric heat lamps and mirrored walls make it seem like a tropical jungle. When the Persian finds a release switch, they escape down into Erik's wine cellar, only to find that the barrels there are not filled with wine, but with enough gun powder to blow up half of Paris.

Above them, Christine is told to turn one knob if she accepts Erik's proposal and another if she rejects him, unaware that the rejection knob will trigger the gunpowder. She turns the one to accept him, and the wine cellar floods with water. At the last minute, Erik has a change of heart and saves Raoul and the Persian from drowning.. Erik goes to the Persian while he is recuperating from that night and says that he set Christine and Raoul free to marry each other and that he is dying of heartbreak. He asks him to place an obituary in the paper after his death, so that the young lovers will know.

The book's Epilogue tells the history of the phantom: how he learned about magic and construction and ventriloquism, how he came to work at the construction site of the opera building, and how he was able to elude detection for so long.

Joseph Buquet

Joseph is a stagehand who has seen the phantom in the opera house's third basement. He is found hanged in the cellar, but when people go to retrieve his body, the rope is missing. Later in the book, the Persian guesses that the phantom killed Buquet with a device called the Punjab lasso.

Carlotta

Carlotta is the opera's female lead, for whom Christine Daaé is an understudy. Carlotta is a technically accomplished singer but does not sing with soul. The phantom threatens her if she goes onstage as Marguerite in *Faust*, but she refuses to be intimidated; as a result, the sound of a croaking frog comes out when she sings.

Christine Daaé

Christine in Sweden was raised by her father, a traveling violinist. As he was dying, he explained to her that he would remain with her and guide her through the Spirit of Music. As a young singer with the Paris Opera, Christine heard Erik speaking to her from behind a wall; she asked if he were the spirit that her father had told her about, and for a while he said that he was. He taught her to sing well, so that, given her first chance for public attention, she sings so beautifully that much of Parisian society takes notice of her. That night, though, she runs into Raoul de Chagny, whom she met and fell in love with as a child; her love for Raoul makes Erik jealous, who does what he can to make her his. He promises her the freedom to leave him but then, unable to let her go, kidnaps her and gives her a short time to consent to marry him before killing her. She tries unsuccessfully to fool him into thinking that she will love him, but he is still moved by her love for Raoul enough to let them leave.

Philippe de Chagny

Forty-one-year-old Count de Chagny, whose given name is Phillippe-Georges-Marie, is the oldest of his family and since the deaths of his parents has been responsible for one of the oldest families in Europe, which includes his brother Raoul, who is almost half his age. He disapproves of his brother's romance with Christine Daaé, so that when she disappears from the opera stage Count de Chagny is a primary suspect. Later, he is found drowned in the lake that protects the phantom's house from the outside world, but the phantom denies any responsibility for his death, saying that Philippe fell out of his boat by accident even before any of the lake's traps could get to him.

Raoul de Chagny

As the youngest member of the prestigious de Chagny family, Raoul has been raised by a sister and old aunt. At the time of the novel he is twenty years old and scheduled to go into the navy and, while waiting for his orders, is spending a few weeks in Paris with his brother Phillippe. He sees Christine Daaé on the stage of the opera and remembers her as the little girl whom he met and fell in love with years earlier, when her scarf blew into the water and he dove in to retrieve it. He can tell that Christine loves him, too, but she tries to send him away frequently, worried that Erik, the phantom, will hurt him. He and Christine agree to a secret engagement, but when their engagement becomes publicized the phantom abducts Christine. The novel's last chapters are about how Raoul, with the help of the stranger known as the Persian, infiltrates the phantom's hidden underground house in an attempt to free Christine. They fail, and Raoul is in danger of drowning before the phantom has a change of heart and agrees to let Christine leave with him, even though it breaks his heart and he dies as a result.

Monsieur Debienne

With Monsieur Poligny, Debienne is one of the directors of the Paris Opera who is retiring in the opening chapters of the novel.

Erik

Erik is the name that the phantom of the Opera has taken for himself; his real name is never revealed in the book. He was born deformed, and it was his mother, whom Eric refers to several times, who gave him his first mask. He was born in a little town near Rouen but ran away as a young man, sometimes exhibiting his gruesome looks at country fairs under the title of the living dead man. As a performer, he learned to become proficient as a musician, a magician, and as a ventriloquist. Summoned by a shah to Persia, he designed a palace with hidden panels and trap doors. The shah ordered him executed, to keep the palace's secrets unknown, but the Persian helped Erik escape.

In Paris, Erik was part of the construction team that helped Charles Garnier build the Paris opera house. Because he knows where the secret passageways are, he is able to move about the opera house without being seen. Because he is proficient in ventriloquism, he is able to speak from hidden places and to make people think that his voice is coming from the empty air beside them. And he uses his musical skill to compose a masterful violin opus, *Don Juan Triumphant*, which he has worked on for decades in his home in the opera house's cellars.

As the phantom, Erik demands that the managers of the opera give him an annual stipend and a private box. Erik falls in love with Christine when he meets her. For a while, he pretends to be the Spirit of Music that her father once told her about, and he trains her to become a great singer. When he is unable to make her love him, though, he becomes insane. He kidnaps her and eventually threatens to blow up a quarter of the town with all of the gunpowder he has hidden beneath the opera house. In the end, though, his heart is softened by her promise to love him, and he lets Christine and Raoul go free to marry each other. When he last appears in the novel, it is to tell the Persian that he is dying of a broken heart.

Mme. Giry

The mother of the girl known as Little Meg, *Mme.* Giry is also the attendant of Box Number 5, which is reserved for the phantom. She has never seen him, but she does services for him, like bringing a program and a footstool to the box. In return, he leaves her tips and gifts. When she is fired by the opera's directors, a huge chandelier falls on the audience, killing just one person: the woman hired to replace *Mme.* Giry. She is assigned to deliver money to the phantom, and when the money in the envelope is changed for counterfeit money, the directors threaten to turn her over to the police until they find out that she could not possibly have stolen it. They do find out why she is so interested in helping the phantom; in addition to the tips that he gives her, he has predicted that Little Meg will be the empress by 1885.

La Sorelli

One of the opera's featured dancers, La Sorelli is a diva who expects to be the center of attention. When she dances, the narrator explains, "she appears to be in a tableau so lascivious that it could drive a man to blow his brains out." But she is also presented as a vain, stubborn woman.

Monsieur Lachenal

Monsieur Lachenal is the stable master of the opera house, in charge of the horses that are trained to perform in operas.

Armand Moncharmin

One of the new directors of the opera, Moncharmin has no musical training but is rich and socially connected. His working relationship with M. Richard is threatened when the phantom is able to steal an envelope of money from Richard's pocket. The book's narrator relies on Moncharmin's autobiography, *The Memoirs of a Director*, as a primary source for the events reported in the book.

The Persian

The Persian is a witness of the events at the opera house, whom the narrator interviews about what happened to Raoul de Chegny and Christine Daaé. The Persian is so famous that he cannot be referred to by his real name. He is a shadowy figure throughout much of the story, until the final chapters. Then, it turns out that he has known Erik, the phantom, for years, from the time when he was the *daroga*, or chief of the national police. In Persia, he saved Erik from execution and lost his government position because of it. He knows many of the secrets of the phantom's underground world, having followed him and observed him and once having nearly been killed by one of his traps in the underground lake.

When Christine is kidnapped, the Persian steps forward to help Raoul find his way through the underground world to the place where she may have been taken. In the course of the rescue mission, his advice is invaluable, but he nearly loses his life when the cellar he is in is flooded. The phantom saves him, though, and, after making sure he is all right, knocks him out with drugs and deposits him in a doorway.

Monsieur Poligny

With Monsieur Debienne, Monsieur Poligny is one of the directors of the Paris Opera who is retiring in the opening chapters of the novel.

Firmin Richard

One of the opera's new directors, Richard is an accomplished musician and composer. He is characterized as loving all types of music and all musicians. He is skeptical of the existence of the phantom and hesitates about giving in to his demands. When the money disappears from an envelope that is pinned in his pocket, he and his partner, M. Moncharmin, become suspicious of each other, a suspicion that seems, according to Moncharmin's memoirs, to last throughout their professional relationship.

Madame Maudie Valerius

Christine is staying at the house of *Mme.* Valerius, an old friend of her father. Raoul de Chagny goes to the house when Christine disappears the first time, but *Mme.* Valerius cannot tell him where she is. She is convinced that Christine has gone away with the Spirit of Music.

Appearance and Reality

The fact that *The Phantom of the Opera* takes place behind the scenes of the opera almost automatically draws readers' attention to the disparity between reality and appearances. Leroux gives backstage details, starting with the dancers who line up in the first chapter, gossiping, and continuing on to point out the backdrops and the business arrangements that few opera goers are allowed to see. Un-like most backstage stories, though, this novel also goes into details about the Paris opera house that few of the average workers would be aware of, such as the complicated system of tunnels underneath the building, with furnaces and prisons and hoards of rats and even a lake. Some of these details might be exaggerated from reality, but they are plausible as the reality of the novel. They clearly indicate that, as much as the sets and costumes create a false world on the stage, the opera house that visitors enter only reveals part of the story regarding what it takes to put on a grand spectacle.

The phantom himself is also used as a symbol to represent the ways that reality and appearance differ. The most obvious example of this is, of course, the mask that he wears. When he is wearing his mask, Christine can believe that he is a poor, misunderstood man who has just not been given the attention he deserves. When he represents himself to her as the Spirit of Music, she responds to his musical gift and really does see him as angelic. Once she sees Erik without his mask, however, she is so horrified that she can never think fondly of him again.

In addition to the phantom's looks, however, his whole existence is one big charade. He is greatly gifted, but his talents are in making voices seem to appear where no one is actually talking; in coming and going without being seen; in overhearing conversations that seem to be private; and in making people think that they see things that are impossible, as in when his torture chamber turns out to be a hall of illusions. He is known as a phantom for a reason: no one is ever really sure that he exists.

Innocence

The phantom's anger with the society that has rejected him is balanced in this novel with the simple innocence of the love between Christine Daaé and Raoul de Chagny. Christine's life story is surrounded by the sort of heartwarming and fantastic details that are common in fairy tales. Her father, for instance, is a kindly old soul and an incredibly talented musician. He fills her childhood with the sweet view of the world that is found in folk stories. Before he dies, he tells Christine that she will be watched over by the Spirit of Music, which at first serves to give her comfort but later, as is common with innocence carried into adulthood, causes her to fall victim to Erik, who uses his talent for ventriloquism to make her loyal to him. *Mme. Valerius* is another example of the innocence that surrounds Christine's life. She never questions that the younger woman is doing the right thing even when others doubt her, supplying a level of sweetness and naiveté that reflects on Christine's under-standing of the world.

The romance between Christine and Raoul is particularly untouched by the harsher elements of reality. From their first meeting as children, when Raoul puts his life at risk in service to her as he swims out into the ocean to retrieve her scarf, to their chance meeting years later at the opera house when they recognize each other, they are true to each other. A few times, Raoul questions Christine about her purity, but he always accepts her word that such questions are misguided. Readers believe so firmly in the couple's innocence that, when the narrator has bystanders remark that it is scandalous for them to go into her dressing room together and close the door, it is the bystanders who seem ignorant of the reality of true love.

Horror

This book uses several standard horror elements to make the phantom threatening and mysterious. The most obvious of these is the opera house itself, with its high, shadowy ceilings and miles of tunnels beneath. When Raoul and Christine go up to the roof, they are among the swooping gables and heavy statuary that set the ominous mood in other works, such as *The Hunchback of Notre Dame*. In its cellars readers are introduced to fantastic sights that are hard to believe: legions of forgotten workers who never see the light of day or swarms of rats that are at the command of the Rat Catcher.

The most distinct horror device is Erik's face. Though he is described as having a skin disease, its manifestation gives him the exact semblance of a skull, so that even as a young man he was able to travel to county fairs and bill himself as the living dead man. His eyes, too, are described as glowing in the dark, like a cat's. These details might be unlikely in the real world, but they are not at all out of place in a horror story.

Topics for Further Study

- Examine the history of the Paris

Commune, which Leroux says lived in the jails upon which the Opera House was built. Find out how much the underground life led in the 1870s corresponds to the underground life that Raoul discovers while going to find the place where the phantom lives.

- This story centers on the opera company's performance of *Faust*. Read a version of the Faust story and write a short play in which Erik and Faust meet, telling each other about their common experiences.

- One of this story's conceits is that, through the use of ventriloquism, Erik is able to make it seem as if his voice is coming out of places that are far from where he is hiding. Prepare a report on ventriloquism: its capabilities, its shortcomings, and its greatest practitioners. In what ways would proficiency in ventriloquism help Erik in pretending to be the Opera ghost?

- Study another opera house, either in person or on the Internet. Report on what areas behind and under the stage would be handy for this house to harbor its own phantom.

Narration

The Phantom of the Opera is told from the point of view of a narrator whose name is never given, who is examining the events of the novel thirty years after the fact. The Preface gives details of his search: how he examined the records of the opera library, interviewed people who had been present at the time of the story (including Little Meg Giry and the Persian, whose name is withheld but who proves to be a major part of the action in the book's final chapters), and examined a skeleton found in the catacombs under the opera house, assuming it to be the remains of the phantom. Throughout the course of the novel, this narrator sometimes makes his presence felt, with statements like "I assume" and "we know now that," but for the most part he stays out of the story and relates the facts as a third person narrator would.

There are several ways in which this narrator gives over the telling of the story to other participants. One way is in quoting songs that were sung at the opera while the story was being lived, giving readers a greater sense of immediacy than they would get from a scholarly recap of the events. The most striking example occurs when he gives the narrative over to the Persian in chapters 22 through 26, using the excuse that these are the exact words that the Persian wrote in his memoir of the events. It is significant that, at the height of this suspenseful story, the narrator changes to one of the two people who is actually involved in the action.

Belle Époque

The long stretch of time between the collapse of the empire of Napoleon III in 1871 and the start of the First World War in 1914 was a relative peaceful and prosperous period for France. Napoleon, like his predecessor Napoleon Bonaparte, had sought to remake Paris on a grand scale, restructuring its centuries-old layout and adding outlying provinces to the city proper. He had also, however, tried to leave his mark as a great military leader, which ended up in his defeat by the Prussians. The fall of the emperor was followed by a four-year period of political anarchy, marked by the uprising known as the Paris Commune (discussed in *The Phantom of the Opera* for the rebels who hid under the tunnels under the opera house). Stability was established under the Third Republic, which came to power in 1875, the same year that the magnificent opera house designed by Charles Garnier was completed.

During the final decades of the nineteenth century and the first decade of the twentieth, Paris saw a burst of technology that was integrated into ordinary daily life with ease. Electric lighting became available in the early 1880s and spread quickly; in the 1890s, automobiles became available; and, just before the turn of the century, the first moving pictures were exhibited. The 1900 Paris Expo, a large party to herald in the twentieth century, hosted nearly fifty-one million visitors: more than the population of the entire country. While France had spent much of the nineteenth century under the rule of Napoleon and his heir, Paris entered the twentieth century as one of the world's great capital cities. This period was known as the Belle Époque, also called the Banquet Years or the Miraculous Years.

Popular Entertainment

When *The Phantom of the Opera* was published in 1910, opera was still a popular diversion in Paris, but other forms of entertainment were more accessible to the masses. The theater world was all overshadowed by the genius of Sarah Bernhardt, one of France's most popular actresses, who started her career in the 1860s at the Comédie Française, the national theater company. Even more threatening to the high prices and formality of the opera was the ascent of the motion picture. Though Americans usually credit Thomas Edison with inventing movies in 1893, his kinetoscope projector was limited to one viewer at a time in a small booth. The first motion picture theater opened in Paris in 1895, using a process that was developed by two French brothers, Louis and Auguste Luminière. The Luminière method became the standard that was to be used in motion picture projection for decades. When this novel was published, the city of Paris already had over thirty-five movie theaters.

While motion pictures made shows available to the people who could not afford tickets to the opera or even to the theater, there were also a number of low-budget music venues that could be enjoyed for very little money. Paris had a tradition of being an artists' city and in particular a city for starving artists, and these artists frequented music halls and provided the talent for their stages. The majority of Parisians, to say nothing of the rest of the world, had never stepped foot inside of the opera house, and learned of its intriguing design through Gaston Leroux's novel.

Critical Overview

It is unlikely that Gaston Leroux's novel *The Phantom of the Opera* would be read today if it were not for the ways that other artists have adapted it to visual media. When Leroux's story first appeared as a newspaper serial in 1909, it was popular enough to be carried in papers in France, Great Britain, and the United States, but the subsequent release as a novel was only modestly successful. It was considered just another thrill story by a competent writer who churned out entertainment stories for a living. The book fell out of print quickly. In 1925, however, while looking for a film vehicle to match the success that he had just had with Lon Chaney in *The Hunchback of Notre Dame*, film producer Carl Laemmle purchased the rights to *The Phantom of the Opera*. The film took great liberties with Leroux's story, but it was a great success, a groundbreaking horror film, and its following continued over the decades and stirred interest in the novel that spawned it.

Modern audiences are familiar with the story of the phantom through the immensely popular stage musical, written by Andrew Lloyd Weber. That play opened in London in October of 1986 and as of 2004 had not yet closed, making it as of that year the second-longest running musical in the history of the theater (after Weber's own *Cats*).

Compare & Contrast

- **1880:** Transportation within Paris is by horse carriage; for cross-country trips, the locomotive is available.

  1910: In the year following the first flight across the English Channel by Louis Blériot, Parisians realize that the age of aviation has arrived. Automobiles are common on Parisian streets.

  Today: Paris's streets, designed in the 1870s, are choked with automobile traffic. For travel on the continent, the TGV, or bullet train, travels at speeds often exceeding 186 miles per hour.

- **1880:** Paris is the artistic center of the world, home to impressionist painters such as Alfred Sisley, Auguste Renoir, Edouard Manet, Edgar Degas, and Paul Cézanne.

  1910: Paris is the home of the influential and challenging Cubist artistic movement, promoted by painters such as Pablo Picasso and Georges Braque.

  Today: The best-known Parisian artists, such as Jean-Marc Bustamante and Sophie Calle, are photographers.

- **1880:** The Garnier Opera building is less than five years old and is revered as an architectural triumph.

  1910: At the advent of the age of Modernism, the Garnier Opera building is seen as an ornate and almost gothic structure.

  Today: The Garnier Opera building is considered to be one of Paris's most important cultural landmarks.

- **1880:** Interior light is provided by open gas flames, lanterns, or candles.

  1910: Large gathering places such as the opera are lit with incandescent lighting.

  Today: Lighting of stage productions such as operas has become an art form in and of itself.

One reason that the novel is so seldom discussed on its own terms is that its story is, in the words of Leonard Wolf, who edited a contemporary, annotated edition, a "strange sort of masterpiece." Wolf points out the conventions of gothic fiction, such as the perils faced by the young, beautiful heroine, pursued "from one cold, dark, dank, and macabre place to another by a tall, dark stranger who is infinitely more interesting than the good-looking and (often) wealthy or titled young hero who rescues her." While many readers have dismissed the book as a hack job, Wolf credits

Leroux with weaving "a tapestry of myth that frequently feels both complex and moving."

In his 2002 study titled *The Undergrounds of "The Phantom of the Opera": Sublimation and the Gothic in Leroux's Novel and Its Progeny*, Jerrold E. Hogle shows that it is in fact possible to give serious critical consideration to the phantom's story. Heavy on psychological and sociological interpretation, Hogle's book observes aspects of the story that have never been noted before. His discussion of the underground catacombs, for example, is common of the tone of the whole book: "As both the principle creditor and himself a debtor in this novel, Leroux's phantom thus occupies yet another symbolic position with many layers, this time in the way the book exposes and disguises the economic roots behind a world of simulation." It is notable that, while taking Leroux's work seriously, still the majority of Hogle's book is concerned with adaptations, from the silent film to the stage musical.

What Do I Read Next?

- In his entertaining 1993 novel *The Canary Trainer*, Nicholas Meyer, writing as Sherlock Holmes's confidant Dr. Watson, has Holmes interact with characters from Leroux's novel, as he tries to capture the opera ghost.

- There are many comparisons to be made between the story of the phantom and Mary Shelley's 1818 novel *Frankenstein*, which also deals with an outcast from society. In Shelley's novel, though, the philosophical questions of what it means to be human are much more significant.

- The costume ball with the mysterious death's head figure in attendance is an almost exact copy of the scene Edgar Allan Poe used in his short story "The Masque of the Red Death." This story is available in most anthologies of Poe's works, including the one published by the Library of America.

- Readers who enjoy Leroux's style might want to read more of his writings. His 1907 detective novel *The Mystery of the Yellow Room*, which was one of his most popular works during his lifetime, is available in a 2002 release from Indypublish.com. Also, a number of his macabre stories were collected in *The Gaston Leroux Bedside Companion: Weird Stories by the Author of the "Phantom of the Opera,"* but as of 2004 this collection was out of print.

- This novel is closely associated with Victor Hugo's *The Hunchback of Notre Dame*. Like Leroux's Erik, Hugo's Quasimodo is a deformed genius who occupies the hidden spaces of a grand Parisian building, pining for the beautiful woman whom he loves. Hugo's novel was available as of 2004 in a Tor Classics edition.

- Robert Louis Stevenson's 1886 novel *Dr. Jekyll and Mr. Hyde* is similar to the tale of the phantom in that it takes place in the late Victorian era and in mostly urban settings, mostly at night.

Sources

Hogle, Jerrold E., *The Undergrounds of "The Phantom of the Opera,"* Palgrave, 2002, p. 117.

Wolf, Leonard, "Introduction," in *The Essential "Phantom of the Opera,"* edited by Leonard Wolf, Plume, 1996, pp. 2–3.

Further Reading

Johnson, James H., *Listening in Paris: A Cultural History*, University of California Press, 1996.

> Focused on the history of silence in the concert hall and opera house, this book gives a good sense of the cultural tendencies of opera goers at the time of the novel.

Perry, George, *The Complete "Phantom of the Opera,"* Henry Holt, 1991.

> Though focused on the London musical, this book is filled with information about the novel and about the Paris opera house.

Skinner, Cornelia Otis, *Elegant Wits and Grand Horizontals*, Houghton Mifflin, 1962.

> Skinner examines the social life of uppercrust Parisian society during the Belle Époque. These are the people who would have made up the opera audience during the time that this story takes place.

Zizek, Slavoj, "Grimaces of the Real, or When the Phallus Appears," in *October*, Vol. 58, Fall 1991, p. 46.

> This analysis examines the correlation in some folk traditions

between the size of a man's nose and his masculinity and the implications of this theory on Erik's physical deformity.